The Passion of Greed

Greed starts out by being a hobby, transitioning to a passion, then transitions to a final stage of addiction. This book talks about greed as an addiction and how a human with morals can overcome it. My name is Shazir Mucklai and I wrote this book to help the 99% of America overcome this addiction.

Greed has ruined many Americans, and it continues to do so. Greed is the reason why millions of Americans lost their homes, it is the reason why scandals erupt, and it is the reason why we can't prosper. Greed has not only ruined the one percent but it has gone and ruined millions of selfless human beings who are out to make a decent living for themselves.

The world used to be a society filled with people not out to be better than others but to maintain their own lifestyles, today it's just a simple "keeping up with the Joneses," striving to be better than our counterparts, to be better than our neighbors and even our own family members.

This is just part of a simple lifecycle; you go to school, then college, then you get a job, retire on social security and die. Within these stages you, you slowly transition from one part of the path to the other crawling, walking, jogging, and then finally running to beat each and every single one whether it be shooting them or killing their confidence. At one point we become so self absorbed we even try to beat our closest peoples.

In the end we are so devious we kill each other like cockroaches and the ironic part is that we all end up being eaten by cockroaches. Greed is such a vital principle to human existence, but of course you could indefinitely urge that without greed we would all be hopeless ants with only one queen.

This book represents a view that is not only mine but it is prevalent in all religions from the Quran to the Torah to the Bible all religions hold a vital concept when involving greed, they all say not to be lured into the trap.

This book not only talks about greed but it then extends to include personal finance; which includes stocks, real estate, saving, and spending. This is all while maintaining a healthy and hopefully wealthy lifestyle and discouraging greed to a certain extent. Personal finance can often be the key to success, if you truly have the will to do so anyone can easily become a millionaire by the age of 40, many estimates say one must be 60 to retain his/her full wealth potential but these estimates are often leave out a vital fact.

The more you save the more you make, hence the more you can spend. Money is a vital concept and if used and estimated correctly one can become very wealthy. Although greed can't be eliminated, and most certainly can be controlled. Controlling greed is not hard it just takes some discipline.

This book features how to deal with specific circumstances in which greed can limit your earnings potential such as the stock market and real estate, and then transitions to broader topics such as family and saving.

Now enough about what this book will be about, the rest is to find out.

The Hobby

The Winners Market

Wall Street is like a game, only with a conscious, instead of being a game that has been already programmed and designed to function a certain way it is consistently being changed, manipulated, and turned to favor the already socioeconomic elite. This creates a virtually impossible way for the middle and upper-middle class to win in this game, and allows the rich to get richer and the poor to get poorer. These days looking at overall trends many people are involved in the stock market as they see a get rich quick scheme involved, what they don't see is the risk involved in it, the stock market can ruin people, but don't get me wrong it can make them rich as well, but it's just unlikely. Greed is essential in the Stock Market, because if discipline isn't there the money wont be there.

You have to remember that the fancy investors we see on TV or the eccentric billionaires we hear of buy this company and that stock did not start out that way, they started from the bottom of the food chain, with of course the exception of a few people, but the point is many investors did not become rich through the stock market but instead through their specific company. As an example take Warren Buffett although he is widely accepted to be a stock market guru, he actually started buying companies very early on, his current company Berkshire Hathaway owns many entities, that was how he got rich, by controlling the company, not speculating. Now this does not mean that average Joe's always lose but there is a good chance that they might.

This creates an unfair advantage for the majority of us who aren't that rich and don't have disposable resources at our finger tips. Just think of it as this, many of this year's billionaires attended an Ivy League school, are business professionals, and are or have been wealthy to begin with, here are a few examples Carl Icahn, attended Princeton University, was born into a Jewish family, and has been fairly rich from the start, Warren Buffett a billionaire who attended Columbia University, and Donald Trump, a billionaire who went to the Wharton School of Business at the University of Pennsylvania, whose father had given him $25 million to start his empire. There are many more examples but all of these names that are mentioned above have some stake in the stock market and whenever they buy into a company, the company generally tends to soar on the day of the announcement. These statements do don't in any way what so ever reflect any views on the people themselves, but this is just a simplistic general observation. Now for the technology sector, Bill Gates attended Harvard, then dropped out and received an honorary degree he was born into a wealthy family, his father is a notorious capital hill lawyer while his mother a school teacher. Next is Mark Zuckerberg who again attended Harvard, then dropped out due to Facebook, his father too was a professional, a dentist to be exact. I went into such great detail to show just how petrifying it can be; the wealthy control everything in our world. And they are greedy but the difference between us and them is that they are disciplined; these guys know when to sell or to stop hedging the stock.

All of the five men mentioned above have had some if not a bunch of impact on Wall Street; this again shows how Wall Street is manipulated. Here's an example would you rather control .0000001 percent of a company or 30 percent, the correct answer is none of the above you would want to control 51 percent if not 70 percent or 80 percent of a company, that percentage or majority shareholder control allows you to have much greater leeway in accompany so you can be manipulative so you can control the company, and so you can make and create any decision you feel is the best for your company. The percentage used above is a bit extreme but in a company similar to Apple that is probably all you could afford to buy while diversifying. Now if you control .0000001 percent of a company that leaves you with virtually no room to do anything. Yet some of us still feel that investing in a technology, financial, or healthcare stock is a "safe" investment. Let's not forget those days when either a random announcement is released or earnings of a company are due. Stocks either leap or plunge enough to make us lose our sleep. Stocks are supposed to offer certainty yet they offer uncertainty; there have even been cases were a stock has stooped down lower than 50 percent after the Food and Drug Administration did not approve the respective company's drugs.

Now let us transition back to the technology sector, as an example let's say you were playing options, which is a horrible idea, but that's completely another story, so you buy ten contracts of AAPI that you have kept for six months already, and let's say you have met your strike price and are in the money. Time flies and you are now getting closer to Apple's earnings but you still don't sell because Apple has had a good rally and every financial media outlet is screaming Apple this quarter will be Apple's finest, and that may stand true, Apple may report better than expected earnings, and the stock might initially skyrocket, but what investors don't know is the guidance they are about to offer.

Selling early is sometimes a key to success in the market; the earlier you sell the less risk there is involved and the more gains are made possible. Yet, you refuse to sell, and then the guidance is released and shares start to plummet. Guidance is often the make it or break it for a stock, it can either push the stock's price forward or let if fall back. What I am trying to say is that you should not allow yourself to be fooled so easily, and this goes without saying buy do not ever put your money in one stock or "basket" if you make this mistake once it can ruin your financial progress for your entire life.

Selling early is sometimes a key to success in the market; the earlier you sell the less risk there is involved and more gains are attained.

Most notable on this case are Carl Icahn and William Ackman were they have attacked companies heads on, Icahn tends to attack the company's management while Ackman simply states they are either scams or they have other issues. Ackman infamously shorted millions of Herbalife's shares. Unfortunately for him, those shares have gone up nearly 120 percent all-in-all he lost tens of millions; in the market today there is tons of market manipulation. The big leagues control everything.

Overall the stock market is a very bad investment if done incorrectly, but can provide staggering returns if done appropriately, even though many of the world's billionaires have made tons if money off of it; such as Warren Buffett, Carl Icahn, George

Soros, and William Ackman, it will not change back when the stock market was introduced it was meant to be a bit riskier than keeping your money in the bank today you can lose half if your net worth in an hour after the closing bell, if you still haven't understood what I mean by that I will repeat it do not invest in earnings.

Relating to the whole earnings pitch, try to never keep a position overnight, unless you plan to keep the company no matter what for more than a year, doing so eliminates a ton of risk that should not be played with. You should only keep a company long-term if you have seen the growth in it; as in it has a great price to earnings ratio, a decent beta, and good revenue buildup over time. Doing this eliminates a bunch of risk on your end, because if you are skeptical about the stock in the first place if it even falls five to ten percent you will sell-out. This brings me to another point, always be confident about your stock, and stick with it.

But the points are only if you absolutely feel you must invest, if you don't need to invest elsewhere where although gains might not be guaranteed at least they are promised. And if you still have the urge to play in the stock market play with buyer sentiment if a stock is trending higher buy it and if you smell even an ounce of terror in the company sell it, many legendary investors say "buy on the dips sell on the rallies."

The dip is often a key to buyer sentiment, this dip is where shares are bought the most, and the rally is where the most shares are sold. Another important thing to remember is that there will always be opportunities. Every second every minute every hour there are countless opportunities where stocks either rise or fall, so do not and I repeat do not be greedy and buy stocks based on little or analysis.

Moving on never hand your money over to anyone, whether it is a stock broker, family, or a best friend; however, the situation becomes different when they are in need, with the exception of the stock broker of course, but as for business never hand your money over, even if the rewards are hefty and promising. Each case and situation differs but these are just some of the general guidelines.

Greed has changed the ways of many people; these same people have ripped off their own family members, their own friends and have ruined their own world, for a hefty short-term reward. This has altered the course of human existence, from the politicians to even the street magician performing or the person playing the coin game. There are many instances through the course of the world's where the passion of greed has killed the person, a few instances include, The Bernard Madoff Ponzi scam, that was called the scam of the century as he not only allegedly but reportedly stole tens of billions from people and human beings just like you and me. And the only reason why people invested with him was probably because he offered a premium of a couple of percent over the industry standard, this is what I mean by being greedy. All in all he was a human and humans make mistakes, whether it not you believe this, there are numerous example of how greed has corrupted fine specimen like you and me.

Don't get me wrong greed is a necessity to humanity, as noted above if greed had not existed I wouldn't be writing this book, and you wouldn't be reading it. Greed exists as an emotion in order to let society function. Greed as a hobby is okay, but greed as an addiction is not. And no matter how severe Greed can be disciplined in the same manner new skill sets are found.

As a young investor I have found that there will be three major recessions in my lifetime and even a depression, I refer to these cycles as the Cycles of the Economy. You see there are cycles that exist as life and death co-exist profitability and unprofitability exist as well. If you closely analyze these cycles, you will find a concurring pattern and trend. Lets explore it, first as it is today the economy is fairly decent people are buying homes, people are selling homes, interest rates start to pick up again, unemployment is at a decent level, and disposable income is a bit above average as well.

Then comes a wave where inflation skyrockets, hence prices escalate and home prices are way out of line, unemployment is very low and things are starting so seem a bit out of proportion.

Finally, in this stage, people fail to stimulate the sky high economy, and in tern failure erupts. The bubble pops and sends the economy into a recession where the unemployment rate rockets up as high as 11 percent and in a depression 15 percent.

Now of course there is much more involved then what is simply mentioned above but this was just the gist of it. But the point was if you are able to recognize these cycles and patterns you can make so much money off of other people's mistakes. Back on March 6th, 2009, share of Bank of America closed the day at $3.14 per share. And is currently trading at $17.43 per share as of March 10th, 2014. Back then shares had gone through a catastrophe after Lehman Brothers and Bear Stearns had filed for bankruptcy, fear had spread like the Bubonic plague. Since that time shares have recovered but are no where near the all time highs of $57 per share, the highs in set in 2007 and 2006. There are numerous examples that correspond to this, including many banks such as Wells Fargo, and Citigroup.

Next, we are moving on to talk about specific industries in general and the unique risk that each one of them possesses.

First off is the infamous pharmaceutical sector, where millions of traders lose money each year, now before I go off on a rampage and make readers upset.

This sector is very good for companies that already have a revenue base built up like Johnson and Johnson, but is horrible for companies who are in the PDUFA stage and who are trying to get their very first drug approved, because there are many examples where the trial has not worked out and shares go tumbling down, in these cases millions of shareholders lose the majority of their stake. As a side note many of these companies, are penny stocks meaning they offer a hefty reward but they also offer a hefty amount of risk. As an example and I would not refer to this as a penny stock, here is Intercept Pharmaceuticals which skyrocketed from a mere $60.28 per share on December 12th, 2013 to $460.21 on March 11th, 2014. These gains have brought investors huge gains of over 680 percent. But the problem is that these gains are very uncertain, the stock usually moves up approximately five percent on any given day which could also mean that the stock could plummet as much has gone up, this stock is very volatile and hence would not be a safe and steady long-term investment. Not saying it's a bad investment it just wouldn't be safe for your portfolio. But instead of investing in the trial phase of the respective company, what you could do is invest in the momentum, usually stocks build up in the months building up to the announcement of the company, stocks tend to move higher on sentiment and momentum. But emphasizing on the subject of this book don't get greedy sell even if a million signs point to the drug being approved sell, sell, sell.

Next is the technology sector, which is increasingly becoming known for its sentiment based trends. A very good example of this would be Facebook who unlike its peers worked hard at staying at its original IPO level of $38 per share, within a few months the stock hit lows near $20 per share, and shortly thereafter it moved up and down until one earnings report hit the market and shares have started to climb ever since. As shown sentiment was key in this as volume and shareholder expectation increased, the stock price started to drive up as well, proving that sentiment means everything.

With all of the above being said, you have to learn to be disciplined and sell at the right time, once you realize the goal you had originally set out for you should immediately sell because anything can happen.

Following the anything can happen guideline, always know not only the company's news but know and abide by the whole market's news. As in lets say Federal Reserve chairman Janet Yellen is speaking at a world conference or a new jobs report is due, do not and I repeat do not buy those stocks which are heavily reliant on news, this intern makes these stocks very volatile and would create a bad situation for you and your portfolio. At times following these events the markets end up 200 points in the red, imagine what this would do to stocks that rely on the overall market sentiment to go up and down for the most part.

Another growing concern these days, is the interference of hedge fund managers and celebrities interfering in the stock market, as an example lets say Person A is a hedge-fund manager lets say I am known as an investment icon in the financial world, I announce that I have initiated a 10 percent stake in stock

XYZ, I bought the shares at $65 per share and announced my position right after the closing bell, in most cases the stock immediately skyrockets, this is obviously good, and in most cases the stock continues to spike higher due to investor sentiment, but now here is where greed comes into play, do not get greedy at this point the worst possible thing you could do for your portfolio is keep the stock. Instead SELL IT! Selling allows you to recognize those profits on paper and build discipline, I can promise you the more you sell when you are willing to do so the more you gains you will realize in the long-term.

Before you go out and start trading you need to follow two very crucial steps; for the first month all you do is watch specific stocks, such as ABC, or XYZ continuously watch them and no other stocks, focus all your knowledge and scope on these stocks hopefully these stocks are less volatile and move but not as much as they should whether it be up or down. Once you finally believe in yourself then open a trading account, and start trading the stock in small quanities, always diversify, again doing so put a limit on your risk so if you lose some in one company it won't ruin your portfolio.

As mentioned above many times Greed starts out by being a hobby, you invest some money here and there in the stock market and other ventures that we will talk about later on, but then this eventually transitions to the later stages such as being a passion and eventually becoming an addiction. If you have the necessary know how you can prevent this passion of greed from occurring, and if prevented long enough this can lead to your success.

Again greed is an emotion, and emotions can be controlled. As a recap, for this section:

- First off try to not trade stocks at all
- Never invest in earnings
- Never hold a position over night
- Never buy a pharmaceutical based on Drug approvals or trials
- Hedge-Fund managers control the majority of the market if they buy into a stock
- And finally never give money to family for investment purposes

Real Estate

Real Estate is very tricky; you have to completely understand what you are doing even if it represents a small percent of your portfolio. Before actually purchasing a property, do not just look at the infamous Zillow Zestimate as it has proven to be often times wrong. Look up the tax values then the average number of houses sold in that respective area within the last couple of months, then look at the price per square foot trending within the past month, and then finally look at the report that comes with the real estate online. Your realtor should know what this is, many people often miss this and it costs then thousands of dollars later.

Fixer upper homes are usually the worst to buy even if they are very cheap, the majority of the time fixer upper's are only for people who are willing to and know how to do the necessary work requires. Do not get greedy and think it will be the world's easiest job, investment homes are usually the same deal

As tempting as it may be do not put a hefty down payment unless you need to or unless you have no other debt. This includes housing and credit card debt. Many and arguably so say that middle class Americans get rich by saving their money and paying rebutting off, this is partly true as you pay everything off your disposable income might increase yet you can only do so much investment wise with a 2000 in extra disposable income, instead focus on your daily job rather than cutting expenses, of course this is subject to a bunch if debate and is very controversial.

As many of my fellow financiers believe debt consolidation is key, when it come to paying debt off. You may be thinking, how does greed relate to any of this. I have known numerous example were people have lost everything they have in a matter if days they have pulled money from their credit cards and have invested it all whether it be in a local real estate property or the deadly stock market these are two of the biggest no no's as this can alter your or your family's well being.

Greed comes into play when you begin to either excessively purchase real estate beyond your means or when you refuse to sell. A man once said, "no one wants to sell when they are making money but want to sell when they are not making money" this very true as many people's net worth is in their home itself. In fact the majority of Americans do not do anything besides their daily job.

Excessively buying can also function as an addiction because the more you buy, if things do not go the way you want them to, losses will skyrocket, and eventually you will hit the point of no return, where debt is far greater than owners equity. This theory is also inline with over expansion, expanding is always good as it means you have the financial ability to continue to grow your business, but when you buy too much at once, that's when we have a problem. At that point two major things can happen; one being you starts to lose focus on your business and everything starts to fall because management is too little and you are the only one running the company. The second point, and this is where things start to get ugly, is where your debt increases, whilst sales fall, this in tern can create a huge mess and can even ultimately prohibit you from ever expanding again.

Don't get me wrong but wouldn't you rather invest in a fairly large strip center or a business rather than a small condominium or residential property? In the beginning like all financiers; invest, invest, invest in small properties learn the basics, but then start transition to bigger and better properties. And above all remember to sell, then buy and then sell again. Remember this cycle as it is a cycle to success. Just look at the top 1 percent, all they do is sell, they sell millions of shares of their company to guarantee their profits, otherwise stocks fluctuate so much they might even lose half their net worth in a year. It has happened before to many smart individuals. This is why when you sell you retain if not all of the potential profits the majority of them, when you sell the business, property, or entity are profiting fairly well. If you remember this it can be very helpful, but if you forget it can haunt you forever.

As a recap for this section:

- Buy a small residential to start off with
- Transition to commercial complexes
- Never over expand

www.ingramcontent.com/pod-product-compliance
Lightning Source LLC
Chambersburg PA
CBHW051305170526
45165CB00004B/1857